YOUR PERSONAL TRAINER'S SECRET RECIPE BOOK

Marla B. Footer, R.N.
Ed Gaut, C.P.F.T.

WILLOW CREEK PUBLICATIONS

Published by **Willow Creek Publications**
A division of Gaucas, Inc.
P.O. Box 86032
Gaithersburg, MD 20886

Cover photograph copyright © 1995 by Ken Graham. Used by permission.

Egg Beaters recipes copyright © by Nabisco, Inc. Used by permission. Egg Beaters and Fleischmann's are registered trademarks of Nabisco, Inc.

This publication is sold with the understanding that the publisher is not engaged in rendering medical advice. Consult your physician before beginning a diet and/or exercise program.

ISBN: 0-9640945-7-6
Library of Congress Catalog Card Number: 95-060576

To Our Clients
Whose newfound enthusiasm for fitness keeps reinforcing our own

Your Personal Trainer's Secret Recipe Book

Table of Contents

Your Personal Trainer's Secret Recipe Book

Acknowledgment

This book is a direct result of our clients' desires to be the best they can be. As all trainers should, we try to educate our clients, so they know the whys and hows of total fitness. In this book, we have not only included our favorite recipes. We have also included answers to the most common questions asked of us about exercise and nutrition. As all of our clients know, we always stress that fitness is a lifetime commitment. This book is a great reminder of that. Read on and stay fit.

A major thanks to those who had a hand in this project: Joan and Alan Hayman for the use of their beautiful home and kitchen; Jeff Jackson for making us look good and supporting us through the last couple of years; the people at Nabisco for allowing us to use their Egg Beaters recipes; our parents, Eddie and Rosita Gaut and Bill and Marilyn Burns, for their continued love and support; Marla's children, Kimberly, Brian, and Scott, for their hard work in eating the test recipes; Bob McCann for his continuing support and valuable advice; and finally a very special thanks to David Cracas, our Publisher at Willow Creek Publications, for shepherding this book through numerous drafts and for his patience in dealing with our hectic schedules. If this book is a success, it is due in large part to his efforts. To all of them and all of you, thanks again.

Marla and Ed

Fitness Tip #1:
Stop Making Excuses

There are a lot of fitness products on the market today which claim they will make you fit instantly and easily without a lot of effort on your part. Do not believe it. Nothing worth doing is easy. This is as true of getting into shape as it is of anything else. Fitness requires time. It requires effort. It requires patience. And, most of all, it requires a commitment by you to changing your body and your life.

The best personal trainer in the world cannot force you to get into shape. You have to make a conscious decision to change. No one said staying in shape would be easy. If it were, everybody would be fit.

A common excuse we hear from our clients is that they just do not have enough time to exercise. We understand that people have hectic schedules and that there never seem to be enough hours in the day to do what needs to be done. If you have decided to make your health a priority, however, you must exercise regularly. The good news is that people who exercise regularly sleep more soundly at night and have more energy during the day. This means that taking the time to exercise will actually save you time by allowing you to get things done more quickly.

While becoming fit is not easy, it is not impossibly hard either. Becoming fit does not require huge changes in your lifestyle. You do not have to live in the gym and subsist on granola and tofu. What it does require are a series of relatively minor changes—increasing aerobic activities, starting some weight training, reducing fat in your diet—which you make and then stick with over time.

Fitness is a process. All the various elements in this process have to be included in order to obtain total fitness. The first step in the process is making a commitment to becoming and staying fit. *Stop making excuses and do it now.*

Appetizers

Crab Spread

1	pound crab meat
¾	cup non-fat mayonnaise
¼	teaspoon minced garlic
1	tablespoon white vinegar
1	cup celery, finely chopped
1	small red onion, finely chopped
1	small jar pimientos, finely chopped

In a bowl, mix crab meat, mayonnaise, garlic, vinegar, celery, onion, and pimientos.

Serve on fat-free crackers or Melba toast.

Calories per serving: 117   Grams of fat per serving: 1

Makes 4 servings

Low-Fat Hummus

Minutes

1	can of chickpeas, drained
2	tablespoons minced garlic (from jar)
3	tablespoons lemon juice
1	tablespoon tahini
	Pita bread, optional

In a bowl, mash chickpeas.

Mix in garlic, lemon juice, and tahini.

Chill mixture. Serve with pita bread.

Calories per serving: 125   Grams of fat per serving: 3

Makes 4 servings

Black Bean Dip

15 Minutes

1	can black beans
1	jar salsa (mild or hot)
1	red pepper, chopped
1	yellow pepper, chopped
1	red onion, chopped

Fat-free corn or flour chips*, optional

In a bowl, mix beans, salsa, peppers, and onion.

Chill mixture. Serve with fat-free corn or flour chips or pita bread.

*You can make your own fat-free corn or flour chips by baking corn or flour tortillas in an oven at 350°F until crispy.

Calories per serving: 130   Grams of fat per serving: 1

Makes 4 servings

Pita Pizza

20 Minutes

4	pita breads
1	jar pizza sauce
2	tomatoes, diced
8	mushrooms, sliced
1	onion, diced
1	package shredded fat-free mozzarella cheese

Preheat oven to 450°F.

Cut each pita bread open so as to create two complete circles.

Spread sauce on each half.

Add tomatoes, mushrooms, and onions.

Sprinkle with mozzarella cheese.

Bake at 450°F for 10 minutes.

Calories per serving: 192   Grams of fat per serving: 2

Makes 4 servings

Potato Skins

4 large potatoes

Salt, ground black pepper, non-fat cooking spray, and Parmesan cheese

Bake or microwave potatoes until soft.

Cut potatoes in half and scoop out insides.

Lightly spray potato skins with non-fat cooking spray.

Sprinkle with salt and pepper to taste.

Place potato skins under broiler for 10 minutes or until they start to brown.

Sprinkle with Parmesan cheese.

Put back under broiler until golden brown.

In a bowl, mix potato insides, 2 egg whites, 1 teaspoon water, salt and pepper to taste, 1 teaspoon minced onion, ½ teaspoon garlic powder. Flatten into cakes and broil with potato skins.

Calories per serving: 50   Grams of fat per serving: 0

Makes 8 servings

Hot and Spicy Shrimp

1	lime
2	garlic cloves, minced
1	teaspoon salt
1	teaspoon light olive oil
¼	teaspoon dried cilantro leaves
¼	teaspoon crushed red pepper
1	pound shrimp, shelled and cleaned

In a saucepan, heat 1 teaspoon of lime juice (from the lime), 1 teaspoon of grated lime peel (also from the lime), garlic, olive oil, red pepper, cilentro, and salt.

Set mixture aside for 10 minutes.

In a separate saucepan, boil shrimp for 6 minutes or until done.

Drain shrimp. Add lime mixture and toss.

Let sit for 15 minutes before serving.

Calories per serving: 140   Grams of fat per serving: 3

Makes 4 servings

Fitness Tip #2:
Eat Less More Often

One of the things we have discovered as personal trainers is that most people consume only one or two meals per day. Frequently, new clients inform us that they do not eat breakfast, rarely have lunch, and then eat a large dinner. This means that clients often go twelve to fourteen hours between meals.

Your body does not know that there are restaurants and supermarkets on every corner. When you deprive your body of food, it starts worrying about starvation. The next time you eat, it protects itself from future starvation by storing excess energy. This excess energy is stored in the form of fat. So, by not eating for fifteen, ten, or even five hours, you are actually conditioning your body to store excess calories as fat.

That is the primary reason that "diets" fail. You should never try to lose weight by eating less frequently or skipping meals. What you should do is eat more frequently. Instead of eating two or three large meals during the day, try eating four or five slightly smaller meals. In other words, eat less food more often. Even without changing anything else about your diet, over time, eating more regularly will help reduce the amount of fat stored by your body as well as maintain your energy level throughout the day.

Soups

Clam and Potato Chowder

2	slices low-fat bacon, chopped
2	green onion, chopped
4	medium potatoes, peeled and diced
3	tablespoons all-purpose flour
2	cups bottled clam juice
2	cans minced clams (or 2 cups fresh clams, shelled and minced)
2	tablespoons white cooking wine
¾	teaspoons salt
½	teaspoon ground white pepper
1	cup evaporated skim milk

Shallots, chopped, for garnish

In a large saucepan, saute bacon until crisp. Drain off excess grease.

Add green onion and potatoes. Saute for a few minutes.

Sprinkle with flour, salt, and pepper. Add clam juice, wine, and skim milk. Stir to blend.

Add clams. Simmer over low heat, stirring frequently for 30 minutes.

Calories per serving: 165   Grams of fat per serving: 2

Makes 4 servings

Black-Eyed Pea Soup

1	can stewed tomatoes
¼	teaspoon coarsely ground pepper
2	small yellow squash, chopped
2	medium onions, chopped
1	zucchini, chopped
4	carrots, chopped
1	can chicken broth, defatted or low-fat
2	(16 ounce) cans black-eyed peas, rinsed and drained

In a saucepan sprayed with non-fat cooking spray, saute carrots and onions, stirring frequently, until almost tender.

Add zucchini and yellow squash. Cook everything until tender.

Stir in pepper, chicken broth, stewed tomatoes. Add peas and 3 cups of water.

Heat to boiling. Reduce heat, and simmer for 30 minutes.

Calories per serving: 212   Grams of fat per serving: 1

Makes 4 servings

Red and White Bean Chili

1 pound ground turkey breast
1 can red kidney beans
1 can white beans
1 large white onion, chopped
1 can tomato paste
1 teaspoon dried oregano
1 teaspoon chili powder
4 garlic cloves, minced
1 medium red pepper, chopped
1 medium green pepper, chopped
1 cup celery, chopped
¾ cup water
1 large can diced tomatoes with liquid
1 teaspoon brown sugar

Saute turkey and onions until turkey is cooked and onions are clear. Drain off grease.

Stir in garlic, peppers, and celery. Cook for about 5 minutes.

Add beans, tomato paste, oregano, chili powder, water, tomatoes, and brown sugar.

Bring to boil. Reduce heat, cover, and simmer for 30 minutes.

Calories per serving: 375   Grams of fat per serving: 9

Makes 6 servings

Tomato and Curry Soup

1	**can whole tomatoes, chopped**
½	**cup white onion, chopped**
½	**teaspoon minced garlic**
1	**can chicken broth**
¾	**teaspoon curry powder**

Salt, pepper, and parsley for garnish

In a saucepan, saute onion in two tablespoons water.

Add garlic, curry powder, and salt and pepper to taste. Stir well.

Add chicken broth and tomatoes.

Bring to a boil. Reduce heat, and simmer 10 minutes.

Let cool. Pour into blender, and blend until smooth.

Garnish with parsley

Serve hot or cold.

Calories per serving: 57   Grams of fat per serving: 1

Makes 4 servings

Gazpacho

1	large can V-8 juice
1	cup red wine
3	tablespoons tarragon vinegar
1	small bottle of seltzer water
½	cup chicken broth
1	jar pimientos, chopped
2	cucumbers, chopped
1	green pepper, peeled, seeded, and chopped
1	medium onion, chopped
6	ripe tomatoes, chopped
4	stalks celery, chopped

Croutons, optional

Combine juice, wine, vinegar, seltzer water, chicken broth, and vegetables.

Chill. Serve cold sprinkled with croutons.

Calories per serving: 108   Grams of fat per serving: 1

Makes 6 servings

Vegetable Soup

1	bag frozen mixed vegetables
2	cans non-fat or defatted chicken broth
1	teaspoon minced garlic
1	cup water
1	can boiled white potatoes, drained and sliced

Salt and pepper

In a saucepan, combine vegetables, chicken broth, potatoes, garlic, and salt and pepper to taste.

Simmer for 30 minutes.

Calories per serving: 68   Grams of fat per serving: 1

Makes 4 servings

Fitness Tip #3:
Cut the Fat

There has been a lot of news recently about how the high carbohydrate diets advocated by many fitness experts over the past decade can make you fat. And it is true, if you eat enough low fat, high carbohydrate foods such as breads and pasta, you will become fat. Your body will store any excess energy above and beyond what it uses—and carbohydrates are energy—in the form of fat.

Nevertheless, if you are adjusting your diet to become leaner and healthier, your primary concern should be to reduce your fat intake. Here is why:

1. Fat is stored as fat. While your body will store excess carbohydrates as fat, it can most easily store excess fat as fat. When it comes to fat, your mother was right; you are what you eat. If you do not want to wear it tomorrow, do not eat it today.

2. Fat is more calorie dense than carbohydrates or protein. There are four calories in a gram of carbohydrates, five calories in a gram of protein, and nine calories in a gram of fat. That means there are more than twice the number of

calories in a gram of fat than there are in a gram of carbohydrates. Reducing the amount of fat you consume will automatically reduce the amount of calories you consume.

3. Fat contains cholesterol. The amount of cholesterol in your diet will not directly affect how lean you are or how you look in your swimsuit next summer. But it will affect how healthy you are. That is why most experts recommend reducing the amount of cholesterol in your diet. This can be done by substituting "good" fats like vegetable oils for "bad" fats like butter and lard. And, by all means, do this. But the best way to reduce your cholesterol intake is simply to reduce your fat intake.

Does all this mean that you should eliminate fat from your diet and subsist of shredded wheat and carrot sticks? Of course not. Fat is not only necessary for good health. It also makes foods taste good. And, if there is one message you should take away from this book, it is that you do not have to give up the joy of eating good food in order to stay lean and healthy.

What you should do is limit the amount of fat in your diet. The usual recommendation is that no more than twenty percent of your daily caloric intake should come from fat. For an average diet of fifteen hundred calories per day, that is about forty grams of fat. This is just a rough guide. Now that you have given up counting calories, do not go crazy counting grams of fat. But, do try to keep your total daily fat intake to forty grams or less.

The easiest way to reduce your fat intake is by substituting ingredients. If you are using whole or two percent milk, substitute skim milk. If you are cooking in oil, substitute a non-stick cooking spray or—better yet—a non-stick skillet. Most of the recipes in this book are examples of how intelligent substitution of ingredients can reduce your fat intake without reducing your enjoyment of food. You can do the same with your morning cereal as well as with your own favorite recipes.

So, if you are already eating a low-fat diet, bravo. Keep up the good work. You will reap the benefits with a leaner, healthier body. But, if you have not yet changed your diet, *stop making excuses, and cut the fat.*

Salads

Waldorf Salad

2   medium apples, cored, peeled, and chopped
2   small pears, cored, peeled, and chopped
1   banana, peeled and chopped
2   stalks celery, chopped
¼   cup raisins
1   dozen walnuts, chopped
½   cup fat-free yogurt
1   teaspoon lemon juice
1   tablespoon fat-free mayonnaise

In a medium bowl, combine apples, pears, banana, celery, raisins, walnuts, yogurt, lemon juice, and mayonnaise.

Toss well, cover, and chill.

Calories per serving: 123   Grams of fat per serving: 2

Makes 6 servings

Salads   35

Black and White Bean Salad

10 Minutes

1	can black beans, drained
1	can Great Northern beans, drained
1	cucumber, seeded and chopped
1	red pepper, seeded and chopped
2	plum tomatoes, chopped
¼	tablespoon black pepper
2	tablespoons rice vinegar

In a bowl, combine beans, cucumber, red pepper, tomatoes, pepper, and vinegar.

Mix gently, and chill.

Calories per serving: 120   Grams of fat per serving: 2

Makes 6 servings

Orange, Nut, and Berry Salad

Minutes

1	can whole cranberries
2	fresh oranges, peeled and chopped
1	dozen walnuts, chopped
1	tablespoon balsamic vinegar

In a bowl, combine cranberries, oranges, walnuts, and vinegar.

Mix and chill.

Calories per serving: 68   Grams of fat per serving: 3

Makes 4 servings

Jamaican
Chicken Salad

20 Minutes

2   cups cooked chicken, diced
½   cup fat-free honey-
     mustard dressing
1   teaspoon finely shredded
     lime peel
2-3 teaspoons Jamaican jerk
     seasoning
2   large fresh mango's,
     chilled and sliced
12   cups mixed greens (romaine,
     bok choy, iceberg, celery,
     green onions), cut

In a large bowl, combine mixed greens.

In a small bowl, mix fat-free dressing, lime peel, and jerk seasoning.

Combine dressing mixture, chicken, mangos, and greens.

Calories per serving: 198   Grams of fat per serving: 2

Makes 6 servings

Chicken and Fruit Salad

20 Minutes

2 cups cooked chicken, chopped
1 cup green seedless grapes
1 ½ cups strawberry halves
1 cup celery, thinly sliced
2 cups pineapple chunks
½ cup non-fat ranch salad dressing (or other dressing of your choice)

Salt and pepper

In a large bowl, combine chicken, grapes, strawberries, celery, pineapple, and salad dressing.

Add salt and pepper to taste.

Calories per serving: 162   Grams of fat per serving: 2

Makes 6 servings

Bean Sprout and Romaine Salad

16 large leaves Romaine lettuce
½   pound bean sprouts
3   whole green onions, thinly sliced
2   tablespoons soy sauce
1   tablespoon rice vinegar
1   teaspoon sugar
1   teaspoon sesame seed oil

Clean bean sprouts and place in bowl.

Pour boiling water over the bean sprouts and let stand 1 minute. Drain, rinse with cold water, and drain again.

Place on towel in refrigerator.

In a large bowl, chop lettuce and set aside.

In a small bowl, mix vinegar, sugar, oil, and green onions.

Pour mixture over lettuce. Toss and serve.

Calories per serving: 59   Grams of fat per serving: 1

Makes 4 servings

Tuna and Greens Salad

20 Minutes

1	can tuna in water, drained
1	head Romaine lettuce, chopped
½	can boiled potatoes, rinsed and sliced
2	boiled egg whites, chopped
1	dozen green beans
¼	cup white wine vinegar
2	tablespoons dried shallots
2	tablespoons ginger, chopped
½	lemon
1	teaspoon basil
1	tablespoon Dijon mustard

Steam green beans and set aside.

In a large bowl, mix lettuce, potatoes, and beans.

In a small bowl, combine vinegar, shallots, ginger, lemon juice (from the lemon), basil, and mustard. Mix well.

Add vinegar mixture to lettuce, potatoes, and beans and toss well.

Mix in tuna and egg whites and toss gently. Chill.

Calories per serving: 75   Grams of fat per serving: 2

Makes 6 servings

Orange and Beef Salad

1	head Romaine lettuce, chopped
1	cup fresh orange sections
1	red pepper, cut into strips
1	cup cucumber, peeled, seeded, and chopped
½	cup orange juice
1	teaspoon Worcestershire sauce
½	teaspoon grated orange peel
½	teaspoon ground ginger
¼	teaspoon minced garlic
12	ounce flank steak

Broil flank steak and slice thinly.

In a small bowl, mix orange juice, Worcestershire sauce, orange peel, ginger, and garlic.

Add beef, toss, cover, and refrigerate for at least 1 hour.

In a large bowl, combine lettuce, orange sections, red pepper, and cucumber.

Remove beef from sauce and add beef to lettuce. Toss.

Add some of the sauce to the salad as a dressing.

Calories per serving: 200   Grams of fat per serving: 8

Makes 6 servings

Fitness Tip #4:
Be Aware of Calories

A calorie is a measure of energy in the food you eat. Your body uses the energy in food for everything that you do. Without sufficient calories, you will die. Excess calories consumed, however, are stored by your body as fat. The trick to becoming and staying lean is to consume enough calories to provide your body with all the energy it needs, but not so many calories that your body stores the excess as fat.

The amount of calories your body needs depends on a number of factors including your level of physical activity, your age, and your lean body mass—how much muscle you have. The more active you are, the younger you are, and the more muscular you are, the more calories you burn.

Nobody should consume less than ten calories per pound of bodyweight per day without the advice of a physician. In other words, if you weigh 140 pounds, you should consume at least 1400 calories per day. If you are already lean, you probably want to consume closer to fifteen calories per pound of bodyweight per day.

Whatever your body's caloric requirements,

do not become obsessed with counting calories. Use them as a basic guide to how much food you are consuming. Reducing the amount of fat, sugar, and alcoholic beverages in your diet will automatically reduce the amount of calories. So, if you concentrate on eating lean, healthful foods, you should not have to worry too much about calories. Be aware of calories, but do not let them rule your life.

Poultry

Lemon Chicken with Capers

15 Minutes

4	skinless, boneless chicken beasts, halved and pounded
¼	cup flour
¼	teaspoon black pepper
½	teaspoon paprika
¼	cup low-fat or defatted chicken broth
½	cup sherry
2	tablespoons lemon juice
2	tablespoons capers, drained

Orzo pasta, optional

Cook orzo pasta as directed on box.

In a bowl, mix flour, pepper, and paprika. Coat chicken with mixture.

Brown chicken in a skillet. Remove chicken and place on heated plate.

To the skillet, add chicken broth, sherry, lemon juice, and capers. Stir and thicken with a little cornstarch, if needed.

Pour sauce over chicken.

Serve with orzo pasta.

Calories per serving: 315   Grams of fat per serving: 7

Makes 4 servings

Barbecued Chicken

4   skinless, boneless chicken breasts, halved
2   tablespoon oil
4   tablespoon soy sauce
2   tablespoon lemon juice
1   tablespoon brown sugar
2   cloves garlic, minced
1   teaspoon dried thyme or basil, crushed
3   whole cloves

Ground black pepper

In a large bowl, blend together oil, soy sauce, lemon juice, brown sugar.

Add chicken to mixture and refrigerate for a least 4 hours, if possible, turning chicken occasionally.

Sprinkle chicken with garlic, pepper, thyme or basil, and cloves.

Preheat barbecue grill.

Place chicken breasts on the grill and baste with marinade.

Grill about 10 minutes on each side or until chicken is tender.

Calories per serving: 183   Grams of fat per serving: 4

Makes 8 servings

Oven Fried Chicken

4   chicken breasts
2   egg whites, beaten
3   tablespoons skim milk
½   cup seasoned bread
    crumbs
½   cup potato flakes
1   teaspoon garlic powder
1   teaspoon light oil

Wash chicken, pat dry, set aside.

In a small bowl, beat egg whites and skim milk.

In another bowl, combine bread crumbs, potato flakes, and garlic.

Dip chicken in the egg mixture. Then roll the chicken in the bread crumb mixture.

Repeat procedure for each chicken breast.

Place chicken breasts on a rack in a baking pan.

Bake at 400°F for 35 minutes.

Increase temperature to 450°F and bake about 15 minutes more or until chicken is tender and juices are clear when chicken is pierced with a fork.

Calories per serving: 391   Grams of fat per serving: 7

Makes 4 servings

Turkey Loaf

1 ½ pounds ground turkey
1 cup whole wheat crumbs
(2 slices)
½ cup onion, chopped
¼ cup celery, chopped
1 small can corn, drained
¼ cup fresh parsley, chopped
¼ cup skim milk
2 garlic cloves, minced
2 egg whites, lightly beaten
½ teaspoon grated lemon peel
½ teaspoon ground sage
⅛ teaspoon ground black pepper
¾ teaspoon dried dill weed

Preheat oven to 350°F degrees.

Spray 9" x 5" loaf pan with nonstick cooking spray.

In a bowl, combine turkey, bread crumbs, onion, celery, corn, parsley, milk, garlic, egg whites, lemon peel, sage, pepper, and dill weed, and blend well.

Spoon mixture into pan and shape into a loaf.

Bake 50 to 60 minutes.

Calories per serving: 190   Grams of fat per serving: 5

Makes 6 servings

Turkey Mashed Potato Pie

8 large potatoes, peeled and
cut into small pieces
1 large turnip, peeled and
cut into small pieces
½ cup skim milk
¼ teaspoon minced garlic
1 pound ground turkey
1 onion, chopped
4 stalks celery, chopped
1 small bag frozen corn and
lima beans (or other
vegetables of your choice)

Salt, pepper, and non-fat
or low-fat cheddar cheese,
optional

In a pot, boil potatoes and turnip.
Drain, add milk, and mash.

In another pot, steam corn and
lima beans until tender.

In a large non-stick saucepan,
saute onion, celery, and turkey.

Drain off liquid. Add garlic and
salt and pepper to taste. Add to
turkey mixture.

Spray pie pan with non-stick
spray. Line pie pan with ½
mashed potato mixture. Add
turkey mixture. Spread remaining
mashed potato mixture on top.

Sprinkle with non-fat or low-fat
cheddar cheese, if desired.

Bake at 350°F for ½ hour or until
potatoes are light brown.

Calories per serving: 390   Grams of fat per serving: 5

Makes 4 servings

Turkey Lasagna

1	medium onion, chopped
3	cloves garlic, minced
1	dozen large fresh mushrooms, sliced
1	pound ground skinless turkey
3	cups tomato sauce
2	teaspoons basil
½	teaspoon oregano
1	package frozen chopped spinach, thawed and squeezed dry
2	cups non-fat cottage cheese
8	ounces part-skim grated mozzarella cheese
1	box lasagna noodles

Pepper and nutmeg

In a nonstick skillet over medium heat, combine onion, mushrooms, garlic, and ground turkey. Saute until turkey in no longer pink. Cover pan and continue to cook until mushrooms have released their juices. Then uncover and evaporate juices over high heat. Add tomato sauce, basil, oregano, and pepper to taste. Reduce heat and let simmer.

In a bowl, mix spinach, cottage cheese, and nutmeg to taste.

Cook noodles. In a 9" x 13" baking dish, layer noodles, spinach mixture, tomato sauce, and cheese. Repeat as necessary. Finish with a layer of noodles, a layer of tomato sauce, and a layer of cheese.

Cover with foil and bake at 375°F for 35 minutes.

Calories per serving: 575   Grams of fat per serving: 9

Makes 6 servings

Stir Fry Turkey

15 Minutes

1	pound ground turkey
1	dozen mushrooms, sliced
1	stalks celery, sliced
1	green pepper, diced
1	onion, thinly sliced
1	can sliced water chestnuts, drained and rinsed
¼	cup non-fat or defatted chicken broth
1	tablespoon soy sauce

Chinese noodles, optional

In a large non-stick skillet or wok, saute turkey for 2 minutes over high heat.

Add mushrooms and onions. Saute for another minute.

Add celery, pepper, water chestnuts, broth, and soy sauce. Reduce heat and stir until broth evaporates.

Serve over rice. Sprinkle with Chinese noodles.

Calories per serving: 395   Grams of fat per serving: 6

Makes 4 servings

Fitness Tip #5:
Drink Plenty of Water

Becoming fit involves making a series of relatively small changes in your diet and lifestyle. One of the easiest of these changes to make is to start drinking more water. Water is essential to the human body, more essential than food; a person can survive for weeks without food, but only for a matter of days without water. In spite of its importance, however, most people do not drink enough water.

We recommend that you drink eight to fifteen glasses of water per day. If this seems like too much of an inconvenience, remember that increasing your water intake will not only improve your overall health. It will also help to increase your metabolism causing your body to burn more calories. This, in turn, will help you lose fat.

To ensure that you have water available throughout the day, we recommend that you carry water with you as you go about your daily activities. Here are some suggestions as to how to do this:

1. Keep a bottle of water in your car. With water easily accessible, you will be surprised at

how much you will drink while stuck in traffic.

2. Keep a bottle of water on your desk at work. You are more likely to take a drink if you do not have to keep running to the water cooler.

3. Keep a bottle in your gym bag. By avoiding the trek to the water fountain every time you want a drink, you will save time during your workouts.

4. Take water with you to the movie theater. It is cheaper and much healthier than soda.

5. Find a bottle holder that can be attached to your waist or has an arm strap. This way you can take water with you on your daily walks.

6. Be sure to take water with you when you travel by airplane. The air in airplanes is very dry, and you can become dehydrated quickly during even a short flight.

When you first start drinking more water, you will probably be running to the restroom frequently. Your friends and family may even wonder if you have suddenly become incontinent. Do not worry. Within a week or so, your body will adjust to the increased supply of water. So fill up several bottles and start drinking plenty of water today.

Meats

Beef Vegetable Casserole

1	cup carrots, sliced
1	cup celery, sliced
1	cup turnips, diced
1	box frozen lima beans
2	cups onion, sliced
2	cups red potatoes, thinly sliced
1	teaspoon minced garlic
1	teaspoon pepper
½	pound lean ground beef

Parmesan cheese and salt

In a saucepan, saute beef and garlic. Drain off liquid.

In a casserole dish, mix carrots, celery, turnips, lima beans, onion, potatoes, pepper, and salt to taste.

Add 2 tablespoons of water.

Arrange meat on top of vegetables.

Sprinkle with Parmesan cheese.

Cover and bake at 400°F for 40 minutes. Uncover and cook 15 minutes more or until vegetables are tender.

Calories per serving: 500   Grams of fat per serving: 13

Makes 4 servings

Barbecued Flank Steak

1   bottle honey-Dijon
    barbecue sauce
1   flank steak

    Salt and pepper

Rinse and trim fat from flank steak.

Lightly salt and pepper both sides.

Place on broiler pan. Broil for 7 minutes each side.

Remove from oven and coat with barbecue sauce.

Return to oven and continue to cook for 15 minutes, turning and basting frequently.

Slice very thin at an angle.

Serve with angel hair pasta.

Calories per serving: 385   Grams of fat per serving: 13

Makes 4 servings

Stir Fried Beef

1	pound sirloin, thinly sliced
1	large red onion, sliced
3	cups broccoli, chopped
2	cups celery, sliced
1	dozen mushrooms, sliced
2	cloves garlic, minced
½	cup soy sauce
¼	teaspoon red pepper flakes
½	cup red cooking wine
1	teaspoon ginger
2	teaspoons light oil
1	tablespoon cornstarch

In a large bowl, mix soy sauce, wine, ginger, and pepper.

Add beef. Set aside.

In a large saucepan or wok over high heat, saute garlic in oil.

Remove beef from marinade. Add beef to saucepan and saute until done.

Add vegetables to saucepan, cover, and cook for 5 minutes.

Add cornstarch to marinade and mix. Add marinade cornstarch mixture to saucepan.

Serve over rice.

Calories per serving: 375   Grams of fat per serving: 15

Makes 4 servings

Stuffed Cabbage

1	dozen large cabbage leaves
1 ½	lb lean ground beef
1	cup cooked rice
1	small onion, chopped
1	egg
½	teaspoon thyme
1	tablespoon light oil
2	(8 ounce) cans tomato sauce
1	tablespoon brown sugar
¼	cup water
1	tablespoon lemon juice
	Salt and pepper

Place cabbage leaves in a bowl, cover with boiling water, and let stand 5 minutes or until leaves are limp. Drain.

In a large bowl, mix beef, cooked rice, chopped onion, egg, thyme, and salt and pepper to taste.

Place equal amounts of meat mixture in the center of each cabbage leaf. Fold sides of leaf over the meat, roll, and fasten with toothpicks.

In a small bowl, combine lemon juice, water, and brown sugar.

In a very large skillet, saute cabbage lightly in oil. Add tomato sauce. Stir in lemon juice mixture.

Simmer covered for 1 hour.

Calories per serving: 372   Grams of fat per serving: 13

Makes 6 servings

Pork with Currant Sauce

1	pound pork tenderloin
1	small onion, chopped
¼	cup currant preserves
1	teaspoon flour
½	cup water
1	tablespoon light oil

Salt and pepper

Cut pork into ¼" thick slices. Pound each slice to a ⅛" thickness.

In a large non-stick skillet, brown pork in oil. Remove pork from skillet and put on plate.

In same skillet, saute onion until tender.

In a small bowl, mix flour and water.

Add flour mixture, preserves, and salt and pepper to taste to skillet and stir well.

Bring to boil, reduce heat, and return pork to skillet. Cook over low heat for 10 minutes more.

Serve with mashed sweet potatoes.

Calories per serving: 350   Grams of fat per serving: 15

Makes 4 servings

Fitness Tip #6: Avoid Diets

Diets do not work. In spite of this, the media has led many people to become obsessed and impressed by fad diets and their promise of rapid weight loss. Unfortunately, the weight that is lost from many of these diets is the result of the loss of muscle and water—not fat. In fact, fat stores stay the same or actually increase on many diets, so that it is very possible for a person to have a higher percentage of body fat after one of these diets than before.

What is worse, these diets are frequently unhealthy and sometimes dangerous. They have been associated with and are known to cause weakness, dehydration, loss of calcium and potassium, and even kidney problems. The result is that rather than becoming healthier and fitter on one of these diets, you become less healthy and less fit.

The next time you become excited about the promise of some rapid weight loss diet, calm down for a minute and ask yourself if it really makes any sense to lose so much weight in so little time. You did not get out of shape over-night; you will not get back into shape over-night. Slow, steady weight loss of one to two pounds per week through a sensible diet and exercise program is the safe, effective way to get into shape and stay in shape. So eat healthfully and exercise regularly. *But avoid diets.*

Fish and Seafood

Bouillabaisse

2	leeks, chopped
1	onion, chopped
2	cloves garlic, chopped
1	cup white wine
1	can tomatoes, chopped
2	cans non-fat or defatted chicken broth
1	teaspoon saffron
1	bay leaf
2	pounds fish (halibut, cod, flounder, red snapper, orange ruffe, tuna)
1	dozen clams
1	dozen scallops
1	dozen shrimp
1	dozen mussels
½	lobster, optional
1	package frozen peas
1	teaspoon grated orange peel
¼	teaspoon fennel seed
1	teaspoon Italian seasoning

Dash of salt and cayenne pepper

In a large non-stick saucepan, saute onion, garlic, and leeks.

Add all ingredients except fish and simmer 15 minutes.

Add fish. Cook for 20 minutes more or until fish is done.

Serve with fat-free french bread.

Calories per serving: 275   Grams of fat per serving: 3

Makes 6 servings

Mussels
Marinara

2	pounds mussels, cleaned
1	(28 ounce) can whole tomatoes, chopped
3	tablespoons onion, finely chopped
2	cloves garlic, crushed
3	tablespoons parsley, finely chopped
3	tablespoons basil, finely chopped
2	tablespoons light olive oil
1	bay leaf, crushed

Dash of salt and pepper

In a large saucepan, saute garlic in oil for 2 minutes.

Add parsley and onions.

Slowly add tomatoes.

Add bay leaf, salt, and pepper.

Bring to a boil.

Add mussels.

Reduce heat. Cover and simmer over low heat for 15 minutes.

Calories per serving: 325   Grams of fat per serving: 5

Makes 4 servings

Tuna with Honey-Mustard

15 Minutes

4	Tuna steaks
1	tablespoon honey
6	tablespoons Dijon mustard
1	fresh lemon, squeezed
2	tablespoons tarragon

Dash of black pepper

Mix honey, mustard, lemon juice, tarragon, and pepper.

Place tuna in a broiler pan and coat with honey-mustard mixture.

Broil for 10 to 15 minutes or until fish is spongy, basting frequently with honey-mustard mixture.

Calories per serving: 220   Grams of fat per serving: 5

Makes 4 servings

Citrus Salmon

4   salmon steaks
1   can of grapefruit sections

    Salt and pepper

Sprinkle salmon with salt and pepper.

Separate grapefruit sections and juice.

Place salmon on a broiler pan and broil for 5 minutes on each side, basting salmon with grapefruit juice.

Place grapefruit sections on salmon and broil 10 minutes more or until done.

Calories per serving: 213   Grams of fat per serving: 4

Makes 4 servings

Shrimp and Rice

1 ½ pounds shrimp
1 ½ cups cooked rice
1   medium onion, chopped
1   green pepper, chopped
1   can tomatoes, cut up
1   teaspoon minced garlic
½   teaspoon pepper
1   teaspoon hot red pepper
¼   teaspoon thyme
1   tablespoon flour
2   tablespoons chicken broth

Steam shrimp, peel, and set aside.

In a non-stick saucepan, saute onion, pepper, and spices.

Add chicken broth. Stir in flour.

Add rice and tomatoes. Mix gently.

Cover and simmer for 15 minutes.

Add shrimp, cover, and simmer 10 minutes more.

Calories per serving: 215   Grams of fat per serving: 3

Makes 6 servings

Fitness Tip #7:
Throw Out the Scale

As personal trainers, our goal is to improve the level of fitness of our clients through both aerobic and strength training activities as well as teach our clients the importance of proper nutrition. Every new client we train receives an initial consultation during which we determine his or her needs and goals. The most common goal new clients have is not to get stronger or more aerobically fit, but to lose weight. Everybody is concerned with losing weight, and our clients are no exception.

We genuinely understand the obsession people have with losing weight. What we tell new clients is what we tell you: stop being so concerned with how much you weigh, and concentrate instead on how you look and feel. Do not let the scale rule your life. The process of becoming fitter and stronger involves both losing fat and gaining muscle. Because muscle weighs more than fat, your scale is a very bad measure of your level of fitness. It is possible to look and feel as if you have lost weight even though the numbers on the scale remain the same.

Better indicators of your level of fitness are the activities you can perform and your appearance. Your goal should be to have a lean, strong, healthy body with a lot of energy. So start eating more healthfully and start exercising regularly. *But throw out the scale.*

Potatoes

Non-Fat Fries

4	large red potatoes
¼	teaspoon black pepper
¼	teaspoon paprika
¼	teaspoon chili powder
¼	teaspoon salt
2	egg whites

Cut potatoes into french fry size pieces and place in large bowl.

Sprinkle with black pepper, paprika, chili powder, and salt.

In a small bowl, beat egg whites.

Pour egg whites over fries and toss.

Place fries in a single layer on a cookie sheet sprayed with non-stick cooking spray.

Bake at 400°F for 40 minutes, flipping fries occasionally.

Calories per serving: 232   Grams of fat per serving: 0

Makes 4 servings

Potatoes
Au Gratin

5	medium potatoes, peeled and sliced
3	medium onions, peeled and sliced
1	tablespoon margarine
2	teaspoons garlic, minced
½	teaspoon salt
1	teaspoon dried thyme leaves
3	tablespoons chopped parsley
½	cup evaporated skim milk

Dash of nutmeg and coarsely ground black pepper

In a skillet, saute onions in margarine until soft.

In a shallow baking dish, arrange sliced potatoes and onions in layers, sprinkling garlic and seasonings between layers.

Place thin layer of onion on top.

Bake at 350°F for 30 minutes.

Pour skim milk over potatoes and onions. Increase temperature to 400°F, and bake for another 15 minutes or until potatoes are soft.

Calories per serving: 175   Grams of fat per serving: 2

Makes 4 servings

Twice-Baked Potatoes

4   large potatoes
½   cup skim milk
½   cup shredded non-fat
      cheddar cheese
1   green onion, chopped

Salt and pepper

Bake or microwave potatoes until soft.

Cut potatoes in half lengthwise and scoop out insides. Set potato skins aside.

In a bowl, combine potato, skim milk, cheddar cheese, green onion, and salt and pepper to taste.

Fill potato skins with potato mixture.

Place on baking sheet. Bake at 450°F for 20 minutes or until golden brown.

Calories per serving: 155   Grams of fat per serving: 0

Makes 8 servings

Mashed Potatoes

Minutes

12   **small red potatoes*, cut into small pieces**
½   **cup skim milk**
½   **cup non-fat plain yogurt**

Salt, coarse black pepper, and garlic

Boil potatoes until soft. Drain water.

Add milk, yogurt, and salt, pepper, and garlic to taste.

Mash to desired consistency.

*Can substitute sweet potatoes for red potatoes.

Calories per serving: 626   Grams of fat per serving: 1

Makes 4 servings

Fitness Tip #8: Take a Walk

As you probably already know, changing your diet is only one component of a fit and healthful lifestyle. You also need to engage in some form of regular aerobic exercise. Aerobic exercise is exercise which elevates your heart and respiration rate for an extended period of time forcing your body to become more efficient at transporting and using oxygen.

Regular aerobic exercise has many wonderful benefits including increased lung capacity, increased stamina, and reduced stress. Aerobic exercise not only burns calories which would otherwise be stored by your body as fat. It also improves your body's ability to burn fat, so that your body burns more fat even when you are not exercising.

There are many different aerobic activities you can do. If you are just starting an aerobic exercise program, we recommend walking at a comfortable pace for twenty-five minutes, three times per week. If you cannot do twenty-five minutes of walking, start by doing as much as you can and work up to twenty-five minutes. If you exercise regularly, you will be surprised how quickly you will progress. Once twenty-five minutes of walking becomes too easy, challenge yourself by walking faster or walking up a hill.

We recommend walking because it is a great form of aerobic exercise. You can do it almost anywhere. No special equipment is required other than a good pair of shoes or sneakers. And, unlike running or jogging, walking does not put much strain on your knees and other joints.

If you prefer to take an aerobics class, use a stair machine, stationary bike, or treadmill, by all means do so. Whatever activity you choose, however, be sure to exercise for at least twenty-five minutes, three times per week. The exercise should be intense enough that you are breathing hard, but not so intense that you are gasping for breath. In other words, on an intensity scale of one to ten, you want to work up to an intensity level of eight.

If you are not yet doing aerobic exercise, the most important thing is not the type of exercise you do. The most important thing is that you start your aerobic exercise program today and stick with it. So, if the most exercise you got today was climbing out of bed this morning, go outside now and take a walk.

Vegetables

Eggplant Casserole

1   large eggplant, peeled and
    sliced
1   can stewed tomatoes
4   green onions, chopped
1   cup non-fat cheddar
    cheese

Place eggplant on a baking sheet which has been sprayed with non-stick cooking spray.

Broil eggplant until brown, turning once.

In a casserole dish, layer eggplant, tomatoes, onions, and cheddar cheese.

Cover and bake at 350°F for 30 minutes.

Uncover and bake for 10 minutes more.

Calories per serving: 110   Grams of fat per serving: 1

Makes 4 servings

Ratatouille

2 large eggplants
2 green peppers, chopped
2 medium zucchini, chopped
2 medium tomatoes, chopped
1 medium onion, chopped
1 cup non-fat Italian
   dressing

Cut eggplants in half lengthwise. Remove pulp. Save the eggplant shells.

Coarsely chop pulp.

In a skillet, cook pulp and onion in half of the dressing for 5 minutes.

Add the remainder of the dressing, green pepper, zucchini, and tomatoes. Cook for 7 minutes or until vegetables are almost tender, stirring frequently.

Spoon into eggplant shells. Serve hot or cold.

Calories per serving: 68   Grams of fat per serving: 0

Makes 4 servings

Oven-Roasted Tomatoes

4 whole tomatoes, cored
1 garlic clove, crushed
1 teaspoon light olive oil
4 teaspoons grated
   Parmesan cheese

In a small bowl, combine oil, garlic, and cheese. Set aside.

Place tomatoes in a non-stick baking dish.

Sprinkle tomatoes with oil mixture.

Bake at 425°F for 30 to 40 minutes or until tomatoes are tender.

Calories per serving: 42   Grams of fat per serving: 1

Makes 4 servings

Spiced Squash

1   package frozen cooked
    squash, thawed
1   tablespoon brown sugar
¼   teaspoon ground all spice

    Salt

In a saucepan over medium heat, combine squash, brown sugar, all spice, and salt to taste.

Stir until hot.

Calories Per Servings: 13   Grams of fat per serving: 0

Makes 4 servings

Fitness Tip #9: Know Your Target Heart Rate

The purpose of aerobic exercise is to stress your cardiovascular system to improve your level of fitness. To do this, you need to make sure that you are exercising intensely enough to get the full benefit of the exercise, but not so intensely that the exercise is no longer beneficial—or worse—dangerous. Your breathing can serve as a rough guide to working at the correct exercise intensity level. Make sure you are breathing hard during your aerobic exercise, but not so hard you are out of breath or unable to carry on a conversation.

A more exact way of determining your correct exercise intensity level is to monitor your heart rate and compare it to a target heart rate. There are a number of different formulas for determining your target heart rate. We prefer to use the Karvonen formula recommended by the American College of Sports Medicine. To use this formula, do the following:

1. Determine your resting heart rate by taking your pulse for a full sixty seconds *before* getting out of bed in the morning. Repeat this on two additional mornings, and take the average of the

three measurements.

2. Find your maximum heart rate by subtracting your age from 220.

3. Choose your intensity level. The American College of Sports Medicine recommends that your intensity level should be in the range of sixty to ninety percent. If you are just starting an exercise program, we recommend that you choose an initial intensity level of sixty percent. If you are over age thirty-five or have a heart or other medical condition which might be adversely effected by exercise, consult your physician when determining your intensity level.

4. Calculate your target heart rate using the following formula: Target Heart Rate = ((Maximum Heart Rate - Resting Heart Rate) * Intensity) + Resting Heart Rate. For example, a forty year old man with a resting heart rate of sixty-five beats per minute exercising at a sixty percent intensity level would calculate his target heart rate as follows:

$$((180 - 65) * .60) + 65 = 134$$

If you are doing an exercise which allows you to check your pulse while you are exercising, compare your heart rate to your target heart rate during the exercise. If you are below your target heart rate, you need to increase the intensity of the exercise by walking faster or rowing harder. If you are above your target heart rate, you need to decrease the intensity of your exercise. If you are unable to check your pulse during the workout, check it immediately after the workout, and adjust your intensity level appropriately the next time you exercise.

When it comes to aerobic exercise, more is only better up to a point. If the exercise is too intense, you not only risk injury. The exercise also converts from being aerobic to being anaerobic—meaning your body can no longer take in enough oxygen to support your physical activity—at which time you lose the full benefit of the exercise. So know your target heart rate, exercise at the right intensity level, and get the most out of your aerobic workouts.

Egg Beaters®

Breakfast Burritos

with Tomato-Basil Topping

10 Minutes

1	large tomato, diced
2	teaspoons finely chopped basil (or ½ teaspoon dried basil leaves)
1	medium potato, peeled and grated (about 1 cup)
¼	cup chopped onion
2	teaspoons Fleischmann's® Margarine
1	cup Egg Beaters® Real Egg Product
⅛	teaspoon ground black pepper
4	(8-inch) flour tortillas, warmed
⅓	cup shredded reduced-fat Cheddar cheese

In small bowl, combine tomato and basil; set aside.

In nonstick skillet, over medium heat, cook potato and onion in margarine until golden brown and tender, stirring occasionally.

Add Egg Beaters and pepper; cook until done, stirring occasionally. Remove from heat.

Divide egg mixture evenly between tortillas; top with cheese.

Fold up one end of each tortilla over filling, then fold in sides like an envelope.

Serve immediately topped with tomato mixture.

Calories per serving: 226   Grams of fat per serving: 6

Makes 4 servings

Mushroom-Herb Omelets

10 Minutes

1 cup Egg Beaters® Real Egg Product
1 tablespoon chopped parsley
1 teaspoon finely chopped oregano, basil or thyme (or ¼ teaspoon dried)
2 cups sliced fresh mushrooms
2 teaspoons Fleischmann's® Margarine

In small bowl, combine Egg Beaters, parsley and oregano, basil, or thyme; set aside.

In nonstick skillet, over medium heat, cook mushrooms in 1 teaspoon margarine until tender; set aside.

In same skillet, in ½ teaspoon margarine, make omelet using ½ cup egg mixture.

Portion half the mushrooms over half the omelet; fold omelet and slide onto serving plate.

Repeat with remaining margarine, egg mixture and mushrooms.

Serve immediately.

Calories per serving: 112   Grams of fat per serving: 4

Makes 2 servings

Lemon Poppy Seed Muffins

2 ½ cups all-purpose flour
½ cup sugar
2 tablespoons poppy seed
1 tablespoon baking powder
1 ¼ cups skim milk
¼ cup Fleischmann's® Margarine, melted
¼ cup Egg Beaters® Real Egg Product
1 tablespoon grated lemon peel

In large bowl, combine flour, sugar, poppy seed and baking powder; set aside.

In small bowl, combine milk, margarine, Egg Beaters and lemon peel; stir into flour mixture just until moistened.

Spoon batter into 12 lightly greased 2 ½-inch muffin-pan cups.* Bake at 400°F for 20 to 22 minutes or until lightly browned.

Serve warm.

*For miniature muffins, use 36 (1 ½-inch) muffin-pan cups. Bake for 14 to 16 minutes.

Calories per muffin: 189   Grams of fat per muffin: 6

Makes 12 muffins

Fat-Free
Tropical Shake

Minutes

1   cup Egg Beaters® Real Egg
     Product
1   cup cold skim milk
1   small banana, cut into
     chunks
1   small mango*, peeled and
     cut into chunks (about 1
     cup)

In electric blender, blend Egg
Beaters, milk, banana and mango
for 1 minute or until smooth.

Serve immediately.

*1 cup guava, papaya or
pineapple may be substituted.

Note: Refrigerate unused portion.
Must be used within 48 hours.

Calories per serving: 98   Grams of fat per serving: 0

Makes 4 servings

Sweet Potato Pancakes

15 Minutes

¼ cup all-purpose flour
½ teaspoon dried rosemary
    leaves, crushed
⅛-¼ teaspoon ground black
    pepper
3 cups shredded raw sweet
    potatoes (2 small)
1 cup Egg Beaters® Real Egg
    Product
⅓ cup chopped onion
1 tablespoon Fleischmann's®
    Margarine

Fat-free sour cream or
yogurt, optional

In small bowl, combine flour,
rosemary and pepper; set aside.

In medium bowl, combine sweet
potato, Egg Beaters and onion;
stir in flour mixture.

In large nonstick skillet, over
medium-low heat, melt 2
teaspoons margarine.

For each pancake, spoon about ⅓
cup potato mixture into skillet,
spreading into a 4-inch circle.

Cook for 5 minutes on each side;
remove and keep warm.

Repeat to make a total of 8
pancakes, using remaining
margarine as needed.

Serve hot with sour cream or
yogurt if desired.

Calories per pancake: 127   Grams of fat per pancake: 2

Makes 8 pancakes

Spinach-Cheddar Squares

1 ½ cups Egg Beaters® Real Egg Product
¾ cup skim milk
1 tablespoon onion flakes
1 tablespoon grated Parmesan cheese
¼ teaspoon garlic powder
⅛ teaspoon ground black pepper
¼ cup dry bread crumbs
¾ cup shredded fat-free Cheddar cheese
1 (10-ounce) package frozen chopped spinach, thawed and well drained
¼ cup diced pimientos, optional

In medium bowl, combine Egg Beaters, milk, onion flakes, Parmesan cheese, garlic powder and black pepper; set aside.

Sprinkle bread crumbs evenly onto bottom of lightly greased 8 x 8 x 2 inch baking dish.

Top with ½ cup cheddar cheese and spinach.

Pour egg mixture evenly over spinach; top with remaining cheddar cheese (and pimientos, if desired).

Bake at 350°F for 35 to 40 minutes or until set.

Let stand 10 minutes. Cut into 2-inch squares. Serve hot.

Calories per appetizer: 39   Grams of fat per appetizer: 0

Makes 16 appetizers

Caesar Salad

12 cups torn Romaine lettuce leaves
6 tablespoons Egg Beaters® Real Egg Product
¼ cup corn oil
¼ cup lemon juice
1 teaspoon Grey Poupon® Dijon Mustard
2 cloves garlic, minced
¼ teaspoon black pepper

Grated Parmesan cheese, optional

Place lettuce in large salad bowl; set aside.

In small bowl, whisk Egg Beaters, oil, lemon juice, mustard, garlic and pepper until well blended.

Pour over lettuce, tossing to coat well.

Serve with Parmesan cheese if desired.

Calories per serving: 86   Grams of fat per serving: 7

Makes 8 servings

Broccoli Lasagna Bianca

1	(15 to 16-ounce) container fat-free ricotta cheese
1	cup Egg Beaters® Real Egg Product
1	tablespoon minced basil (or 1 teaspoon dried basil leaves)
½	cup chopped onion
1	clove garlic, minced
2	tablespoons Fleischmann's® Margarine
¼	cup all-purpose flour
2	cups skim milk
2	(10-ounce) packages frozen chopped broccoli, thawed and drained
1	cup shredded part-skim mozzarella cheese
9	lasagna noodles, cooked and drained
1	small tomato, chopped
2	tablespoons grated Parmesan cheese

In small bowl, combine ricotta, Egg Beaters and basil; set aside.

In saucepan, over medium heat, cook onion and garlic in margarine until tender.

Stir in flour; cook for 1 minute. Gradually stir in milk; cook, stirring until mixture thickens and begins to boil. Remove from heat; stir in broccoli and mozzarella cheese.

In lightly greased 13 x 9 x 2-inch baking dish, place 3 lasagna noodles; top with ⅓ each ricotta and broccoli mixtures. Repeat layers 2 more times. Top with tomato; sprinkle with Parmesan cheese.

Bake at 350°F for 1 hour or until set. Let stand 10 minutes before serving.

Calories per serving: 302   Grams of fat per serving: 7

Makes 8 servings

Penne Primavera

20 Minutes

2   cups red, green or yellow pepper strips
1   cup sliced zucchini or yellow squash
1   cup julienne carrot strips
½   cup sliced onion
2   teaspoons Italian seasoning
2   cloves garlic, crushed
¼   teaspoon ground black pepper
2   tablespoons Fleischmann's® Margarine
1   cup coarsely chopped tomato
1   pound penne pasta, cooked and drained
1   cup Egg Beaters® Real Egg Product
¼   cup grated Parmesan cheese

In skillet, over medium heat, cook and stir peppers, zucchini, carrots, onion, Italian seasoning, garlic and pepper in margarine for 3 minutes.

Add tomato; cook for 1 minute more or until vegetables are tender-crisp.

Toss with hot pasta, Egg Beaters and cheese. Serve immediately.

Calories per serving: 288   Grams of fat per serving: 5

Makes 8 servings

Fat-Free Cappuccino Flan

1   cup Egg Beaters® Real Egg
       Product
½   cup sugar
1   tablespoon instant espresso
       or coffee powder
½   teaspoon vanilla extract
⅛   teaspoon ground cinnamon
2 ⅓   cups skim milk, scalded
       and cooled 10 minutes

       **Light non-dairy whipped
       topping and ground
       cinnamon or cocoa
       powder, for garnish**

Combine Egg Beaters, sugar, espresso or coffee powder, vanilla and cinnamon. Gradually stir in milk.

Pour into 6 lightly greased 6-ounce custard cups. Set cups in pan filled with 1-inch depth hot water.

Bake at 350°F for 35 to 40 minutes or until knife inserted in center comes out clean.

Remove from pan; cool to room temperature. Chill until firm, about 2 hours.

To serve, loosen edges with knife; invert onto individual plates.

Top with whipped topping and cinnamon or cocoa powder if desired.

Calories per serving: 120   Grams of fat per serving: 0

Makes 6 servings

Blueberry Bread Pudding
with Caramel Sauce

2	cups skim milk
1	cup Egg Beaters® Real Egg Product
⅔	cup sugar
1	teaspoon vanilla extract
¼	teaspoon ground cinnamon
8	slices white bread, cubed (about 4 cups)
1	cup fresh or frozen blueberries

Carmel Sauce (recipe follows)

In large bowl, blend together milk, Egg Beaters, sugar, vanilla and cinnamon; set aside.

Place bread cubes in bottom of lightly greased 8 x 8 x 2-inch baking dish; sprinkle with blueberries.

Pour egg mixture evenly over bread mixture.

Set dish in pan filled with 1-inch depth hot water. Bake at 350°F for 1 hour or until set.

Serve warm with Caramel Sauce.

Caramel Sauce: In small saucepan, over low heat, heat ¼ cup skim milk and 14 vanilla caramels until caramels are melted, stirring frequently.

Calories per serving: 210   Grams of fat per serving: 2

Makes 9 servings

Chewy Lemon-Honey Cookies

20 Minutes

2 cups all-purpose flour
1 ½ teaspoons baking soda
⅓ cup Fleischmann's®
Margarine, softened
¼ cup honey
¼ cup sugar
1 tablespoon grated lemon peel
¼ cup Egg Beaters® Real Egg Product

Lemon Glaze, optional (recipe follows)

In small bowl, combine flour and baking soda; set aside.

In large bowl, with electric mixer at medium speed, beat margarine, honey, sugar and lemon peel until light and fluffy. Beat in Egg Beaters. Gradually stir in flour mixture until blended.

Drop dough by rounded teaspoons onto lightly greased baking sheets; bake at 350°F for 7 to 8 minutes or until lightly browned. Remove from baking sheets; cool completely on wire racks. Frost with Lemon Glaze if desired. Store cookies in airtight container for up to one week.

Lemon Glaze: In small bowl, whisk together 1 cup confectioners' sugar and 2 tablespoons lemon juice until smooth.

Calories per cookie: 52   Grams of fat per cookie: 1

Makes 3 ½ dozen cookies

Fat-Free Cheesecake

1 tablespoon graham
   cracker crumbs
1 ½ cups nonfat cottage cheese
1 cup Egg Beaters® Real Egg
   Product
½ cup sugar
½ cup nonfat cream cheese
   (4 ounces)
1 tablespoon lemon juice
¼ teaspoon grated lemon
   peel

Sprinkle graham cracker crumbs on bottom and side of lightly greased 9-inch square baking pan; set aside.

In electric blender or food processor, blend cottage cheese and ½ cup Egg Beaters until smooth, scraping down side of container as necessary.

In larger bowl, combine cottage cheese mixture, remaining Egg Beaters, sugar, cream cheese, lemon juice and lemon peel. Beat at low speed 2 minutes. Pour into prepared pan.

Bake at 325°F for 50 minutes or until set and lightly browned.

Cool in pan on wire rack. Chill at least 2 hours. To serve, cut cheesecake into squares; garnish as desired.

Calories per serving: 105   Grams of fat per serving: 0

Makes 9 servings

Fitness Tip #10: Pump Some Iron

It used to be that the only time people ran was when they were either chasing or being chased; in other words, aerobic activity was for survival. Then in the 1970s and 80s, people discovered the benefits of regular aerobic exercise. Now they run, jog, and do all sorts of other aerobic activities just for fun and fitness.

Similarly, people used to lift heavy objects only when necessary to move something from one place to another. In the 1980s and 90s, however, the health community began to recognize the benefits of regular weight training exercise, what the hardcore lifters call "pumping iron." Today, most experts agree that a sensible fitness program should include both aerobic and weight training exercise.

Unlike aerobic exercise, weight training requires some special equipment and knowledge. While there are many excellent instructional books and videos on weight training, we suggest that anyone just beginning a weight training program should, if at all possible, consult a personal trainer or someone else knowledgeable in exercise and kinesiology.

Knowing how to perform exercises correctly is essential not only to getting the maximum benefit from the exercises, but also to avoiding injury.

Having said that, here are some things to keep in mind while you are weight training:

1. Always lift in a controlled manner. Throwing a weight forward quickly or letting a weight drop back quickly not only decreases the value of the exercise. It is also a prescription for injury. Start off with slow motions; two seconds up and four seconds down is a nice pace.

2. Never lock your knee or elbow joints. Make sure that, whatever exercise you are doing, you never fully extend your knees or arms. This will help avoid knee and elbow injuries.

3. Make sure that the weight you use is not too heavy. You should be able to perform at least eight repetitions of an exercise. If not, the weight is too heavy.

4. Make sure that you are working your muscles hard. If you can lift a weight fifteen times with perfect form, increase the weight. Make sure that you are performing the exercise through the full range of motion, and focus on the muscles being worked as you work them. Thinking of what you are doing while you are doing it will help you gain so much more from your workout.

4. Do not forget to breathe. Exhale on exertion, i.e. while lifting the weight. Inhale while lowering the weight back down. When doing

slow repetitions, do not be afraid to breathe more than once during a repetition. Whatever you do, do not hold your breath.

5. Never compromise your exercise form. Lifting with proper form is the key to safe and effective weight training. Remember to position your body so that it is always in alignment; keep your back straight and your abdominal muscles tight. If you are unable to maintain correct form, reduce the amount of weight you are using.

6. Allow your muscles to recuperate between workouts. Muscles grow during recuperation, not during exercise. If you do not allow your muscles to recuperate, you will lose the benefit of the exercise. Muscles need at least forty-eight hours to recuperate. So we recommend total body weight training two or three times per week with at least one day between workouts.

The benefits of weight training are endless. They include increased strength, increased resistance to injury, and increased bone density. And, just as an eight cylinder automobile engine burns more fuel than a six or four cylinder engine even when idling, the more muscular your body, the more fuel it requires and the more calories you will burn even when resting.

Some people avoid weight training because they are concerned that lifting weights will make them too big and muscular. Neither men nor women need worry. Developing muscles the size of a bodybuilder's requires a very deliberate effort above and beyond simple weight training.

What weight training will do is make your body lean and strong. And that is something everyone can benefit from. So find a gym or health club, or get yourself some weight lifting equipment. Find someone to instruct you in correct exercise form. *And start pumping iron today.*

Desserts

Baked Bananas

20 Minutes

4   medium bananas, peeled
    and halved lengthwise
2   tablespoons firmly packed
    brown sugar
1   tablespoon lemon juice
1   tablespoon low-fat
    margarine

Arrange bananas in buttered baking dish.

Brush lightly with margarine.

Sprinkle with lemon juice and sugar.

Bake uncovered at 350°F for 15 minutes, turning bananas halfway through.

Calories per serving: 84   Grams of fat per serving: 1

Makes 4 servings

Apples in Brown Sugar

20 Minutes

¼   cup apple juice
4   medium tart apples, cored and peeled
2   tablespoons lemon juice
2   tablespoons low-fat margarine
2   tablespoons firmly packed brown sugar
½   tablespoon nutmeg

In a heavy skillet, melt margarine.

Add apples, and cook for 5 minutes, stirring frequently.

Sprinkle apples with apple juice, sugar, nutmeg, and lemon juice.

Continue to cook apples until apples soften, sugar melts, and mixture boils.

Calories per serving: 125   Grams of fat per serving: 2

Makes 4 servings

Broiled Grapefruit

1   grapefruit, halved and
     sectioned
4   teaspoons sugar
¼   teaspoon cinnamon

In a small bowl, mix cinnamon and sugar.

Place grapefruit on baking sheet.

Sprinkle cinnamon and sugar mixture evenly over grapefruit.

Broil grapefruit 3 to 4 inches from the heat for 5 minutes or until bubbling hot and lightly browned.

Serve hot.

Calories per serving: 68   Grams of fat per serving: 0

Makes 2 servings

Chocolate-Cherry Yogurt Cake

1   box Devil's Food cake mix
1   pint vanilla non-fat frozen
    yogurt
1   can light cherry pie filling

Prepare Devil's Food cake following recipe on the box but substituting egg whites for eggs.

Soften yogurt.

Cover top of cake with a layer of half the frozen yogurt.

Then layer with half of the can of cherries.

Place second cake on top.

Cover with a layer of the remaining frozen yogurt followed by a layer of the remaining cherries.

Put finished cake into freezer until ready to serve.

Calories per serving: 420   Grams of fat per serving: 1

Makes 8 servings

Tropical Frozen Fruit Drink

Minutes

1	teaspoon coconut flavor
1	ripe peach, pitted
1	ripe banana, peeled
3	tablespoons frozen pineapple juice concentrate
1	cup cracked ice

In a blender, combine peach, pineapple concentrate, banana, coconut flavor, and ice.

Blend on high until smooth.

Serve immediately.

Calories per serving: 110   Grams of fat per serving: 0

Makes 2 servings

Fruit Yogurt Shake

Minutes

¼	cup non-fat plain yogurt
4	strawberries
2	bananas, peeled
¼	cup apple, orange, pineapple, or papaya juice

In a blender, put yogurt, strawberries, bananas, and fruit juice.

Blend until smooth.

Serve immediately.

Calories per serving: 142   Grams of fat per serving: 1

Makes 2 servings

Fitness Tip #11:
Set Goals

If you are serious about getting into shape, we strongly recommend that you set fitness goals for yourself. Goals give direction to your efforts and help keep you motivated and focused from day to day. Otherwise, if you do not know where you want to go, the likelihood of you getting there is slim.

The first step is to set a long term goal. A long term goal is a goal you want to reach in several months. For example, your long term goal might be to get back to an old waist size or to fit into a dress you have not been able to wear recently. Or your long term goal might be to improve your stamina for tennis or to get up the stairs to your apartment without becoming winded. Whatever your long term goal, it should be ambitious but realistic.

Once you have decided upon a realistic long term goal, you next need to come up with monthly short term goals. The short term goals are milestones on the way to your long term goal. They provide you with a regular measure of the progress you are making toward your long term goal. For example, if your long term goal is to lose six inches off your waist in the next six months, a reasonable monthly short term goal would be to lose one inch off your waist.

If you are meeting or exceeding your short term goals each month, you know that you will reach your long term goal. If you are not meeting your short term goals, you know that either your goals were unrealistic or you need to work harder. Whatever goals you set, write them down on your calendar or daily planner and check them off as you reach them.

Once you have established your goals, you need to decide what you are going to do to achieve them. The answers should be a combination of everything we discuss in this book, including diet and exercise. Again, once you come up with a plan, mark the days you intend to exercise on your calendar or daily planner and check them off as you do them.

If you are really ambitious, you can even plan your meals in advance and write them on your calendar as well. This is usually too time consuming and restrictive for most people, however. Simply using low-fat recipes, following the dietary recommendations in this book, and keeping rough track of your daily fat and calorie consumption should be sufficient. But, if you are really ambitious, by all means, create a menu plan. We do.

Whatever your short term goals, stick with them; they will make your long term goal a reality. If you falter one day, get back on track the next. Do not give up even if you fail to stick with your plan for several days in a row. The excuse that there is no point in continuing because you missed a few days is crap. Setting ambitious but realistic fitness goals and then sticking with them from day to day is the best way to reach the level of fitness you desire.

Substitutions

One of the tricks to healthful eating is to substitute ingredients and foods. There are many ways to make food delicious and fun to eat without using large amounts of fat and salt. The recipes in this book are excellent examples. Here are some additional ideas for interesting, healthful, substitutions:

1. Substitute your own non-fat whipped topping for whipped cream on desserts. To make a non-fat whipped topping, beat powdered skim milk with ice cold water adding a little water at a time until the mixture has the consistency of whipped cream.

2. Substitute applesauce for lard or other shortening in cakes, muffins, and non-yeast breads. Start by replacing only part of the shortening. If you like the result, replace more of the shortening the next time you bake.

3. Substitute non-fat evaporated or condensed milk for cream. Do this in your coffee as well as in recipes.

4. Substitute skim milk for whole milk wherever and whenever you can.

5. Substitute a non-stick spray or non-stick pan for oil or butter when sauteing. If you need more liquid, try sauteing in a few tablespoons of chicken broth.

6. Substitute low-fat or defatted chicken broth for regular chicken broth. If you make your own broth, allow it to cool and then skim the fat off the top.

7. Substitute pork or chicken for beef and lamb. Do not buy

ground meat of any kind. Instead, have the butcher trim the meat and grind it for you or, better yet, trim and grind the meat yourself.

8. Substitute non-fat frozen yogurt or ices for ice cream. Frozen seedless grapes also make a refreshing dessert alternative.

9. Substitute egg whites or Egg Beaters® for some of the eggs in egg dishes and recipes which call for whole eggs.

10. Substitute tuna and other meats packed in water for those packed in oil. Rinse tuna and other canned goods before using to remove excess salt.

11. Substitute salad dressings made with flavored vinegars for salad dressings made with oil.

12. Substitute Seltzer water flavored with a little fruit juice for soda. If you are feeling particularly creative, top the drink with a dash of rosewater.

13. Substitute vegetables for meat in dishes wherever possible. Think of red meat as a garnish.

Nutrition Labels

The U.S. Food and Drug Administration has attempted to aid consumers recently by requiring standardized nutrition labels on most foods and food products. These new labels contain a large amount of information. The trick to using them to make wise purchasing and eating decisions is to separate the important information from the unimportant information. Here are some suggestions for doing just that:

1. The first items you should look for on a nutrition label are the serving size and servings per container. Without these two numbers, most of the rest of the information on the label is meaningless. Compare the serving size to the amount of the product you are planning to eat. If the serving size is one cup and you are planning to eat two cups, you will need to multiply all the per serving values, such as grams of fat per serving, by two. Be wary of unrealistically low serving sizes. Manufacturers set serving sizes as small as possible to make the amount of calories, fat, and sodium in a product appear less than it really is.

2. After you know the serving size and have figured out how many servings you are realistically going to consume, take a look at the grams of fat per serving. Most individuals should limit their daily intake of fat to no more than forty grams. Use the grams of fat per serving number on nutrition labels to help you reach this goal.

3. Do not worry too much about calories or grams of carbohydrates per serving. As we have said before, if you concentrate on limiting your fat intake, your caloric intake should take care of itself.

4. After noting the grams of fat per serving, take a look at the number of milligrams of sodium per serving. As with fat, you want to limit your total daily intake of sodium—2400 milligrams of sodium per day is really the maximum you want in your diet.

5. Finally, examine the ingredient list, paying attention to the order in which ingredients appear. Ingredients are listed in descending order of quantity from the ingredient which appears in the largest quantity to the ingredient which appears in the smallest quantity. If salt, fat, or sugar appears at the end of a long list of ingredients, it probably is not too much of a concern. If it appears as the first or second ingredient, however, you may want to avoid this product.

About the Authors

Marla B. Footer, R.N. is a registered nurse, an American Council on Exercise certified fitness instructor, and a mother of three. She has extensive experience in behavior modification and weight reduction as well as in orthopedic and rehabilitation nursing. For ten years, she managed a medical practice where she advised pregnant women on healthy weight control and exercise. More recently, she was director of the "A Better Weigh" weight loss program for the Sport and Health athletic club chain and worked with the "Choose to Lose" weight loss and behavior modification program. She is currently the case manager at the Shady Grove Adventist Nursing and Rehabilitation Center Subacute Care Center in Maryland.

Ed Gaut, C.P.F.T. is a nationally-known personal trainer and fitness author. He and his company, Bodies Plus Fitness Systems, have been featured, among other places, on the cable sports network ESPN and in national newspapers and magazines including *The Washington Times* and *Total Fitness* magazine, the editor of which called his company "one of the fastest growing most multi-faceted fitness units in America." Mr. Gaut is the 1992 Mr. Exercise Competition winner and a 1993 Mr. Fitness World Competition finalist. He is author of *The Personal Trainer Business Handbook*, a guide to the personal training business.

Index

Exercise and Fitness Books
Available from

Willow Creek Publications

Your Personal Trainer's Secret Recipe Book
Quick and Easy Recipes
From Two Of America's Leading Fitness Trainers
By Marla B. Footer, R.N. and Ed Gaut, C.P.F.T
140 pages, 5½" x 8½"
ISBN 0-9640945-7-6
$14.95
Item #CB165

The Personal Trainer Business Handbook
How To Make Money
Running Your Own Personal Training Business
By Ed Gaut, C.P.F.T
140 pages, 8½" x 11"
ISBN 0-9640945-3-3
$24.95
Item #1001

How To Chart Your Fitness Progress
By Joel D. Johnson
ISBN 0-9629387-5-0
$15.95
Item #9009

TO ORDER CALL 1-800-823-3488 EXT 224

Or use order form on next page
Include $3.50 shipping and handling per book
Maryland orders add 5% sales tax

ORDER FORM

FOR FASTEST DELIVERY, CALL 1-800-823-3488 EXT 224

Item#	Quantity	Description	Total

Maryland residents add 5% sales tax _____

Total _____

Method of Payment (check one): ☐ Check ☐ Money Order ☐ Visa/MasterCard/Discover

If method of payment is Visa/MasterCard/Discover, please include the following information:

Credit Card Number _____

Expiration Date _____

Name on Card _____

Signature _____

Ordered By:

Name _____

Address _____

_____

Telephone _____

Ship To (If different than ordered by):

Name _____

Address _____

_____

Telephone _____

Send with payment to: Willow Creek Publications, P.O. Box 86032, Gaithersburg, MD 20886